# Children of Clay

WE ARE STILL HERE
NATIVE AMERICANS TODAY

# Children of Clay

## A Family of Pueblo Potters

**Rina Swentzell**
**Photographs by Bill Steen**
*With a Foreword by Michael Dorris*

Lerner Publications Company ● Minneapolis

Series Editor: Gordon Regguinti
Series Consultants: W. Roger Buffalohead, Juanita G. Corbine Espinosa

Illustrations by Carly Bordeau
Photograph on page 14 courtesy of Mark Nohl, New Mexico Magazine

*This book is available in two editions:*
Library binding by Lerner Publications Company,
 a division of Lerner Publishing Group
Soft cover by First Avenue Editions,
 an imprint of Lerner Publishing Group
241 First Avenue North
Minneapolis, MN 55401 U.S.A.

Website address: www.lernerbooks.com

Library of Congress Cataloging-in-Publication Data

Swentzell, Rina.
    Children of Clay: a family of Pueblo potters / by Rina Swentzell;
photographs by Bill Steen ; foreword by Michael Dorris.
        p.    cm.—(We are still here)
    Includes bibliographical references.
    Summary: Members of a Tewa Indian family living in Santa Clara
Pueblo in New Mexico follow the age-old tradition of their people
as they create various objects of clay.
    ISBN-13: 978–0–8225–2654–4 (lib. bdg. : alk. paper)
    ISBN-10: 0–8225–2654–9 (lib. bdg. : alk. paper)
    ISBN-13: 978–0–8225–9627–1 (pbk. : alk. paper)
    ISBN-10: 0–8225–9627–X (pbk. : alk. paper)
    1. Tewa Indians—Pottery—Juvenile literature. 2. Tewa Indians—
Social life and customs—Juvenile literature. 3. Pottery craft—New
Mexico—Santa Clara Pueblo—Juvenile literature. 4. Santa Clara
Pueblo (N.M.)—Social life and customs—Juvenile literature.
[1. Tewa Indians—Social life and customs. 2. Indians of North
America—Social life and customs. 3. Pottery craft. 4. Santa Clara
Pueblo (N.M.)]  I. Steen, Bill, ill. II. Title. III. Series.
E99.T35S94 1992
978.9'52—dc20                                      92-8680

Manufactured in the United States of America
6 7 8 9 10 11 – JR – 11 10 09 08 07 06

*For Gia and Ta*

## *Foreword*

*by Michael Dorris*

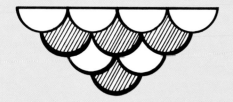

How do we get to be who we are? What are the ingredients that shape our values, customs, language, and tastes, that bond us into a unit different from any other? On a large scale, what makes the Swedes Swedish or the Japanese Japanese?

These questions become even more subtle and interesting when they're addressed to distinct and enduring traditional cultures coexisting within the boundaries of a large and complex society. Certainly Americans visiting abroad have no trouble recognizing their fellow countrymen and women, be they black or white, descended from Mexican or Polish ancestors, rich or poor. As a people, we have much in common, a great deal that we more or less share: a recent history, a language, a common denominator of popular music, entertainment, and politics.

But, if we are fortunate, we also belong to a small, more particular community, defined by ethnicity or kinship, belief system or geography. It is in this intimate circle that we are most "ourselves," where our jokes are best appreciated, our special dishes most enjoyed. These are the people to whom we go first when we need comfort or empathy, for they speak our own brand of cultural shorthand, and always know the correct things to say, the proper things to do.

*Children of Clay* provides an insider's view into just such a world, that of the contemporary Pueblo people of northern New Mexico. If we are ourselves Pueblo, we will probably nod often while reading these pages, affirming the familiar, approving that this tribal family keeps alive and passes on the "right" way to collect clay and make pottery. If we belong to another tribe, we will follow this special journey of initiation and education with interest, gaining respect for a way of doing things that's rich and rewarding.

Michael Dorris is the author of *A Yellow Raft in Blue Water, The Broken Cord,* and, with Louise Erdrich, *The Crown of Columbus.* His first book for children is *Morning Girl.*

*Gia Rose*

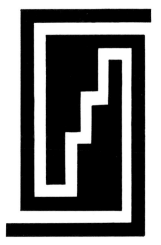

*I*t is an early summer morning in northern New Mexico. *Gia* (Mother) Rose stands outside her house in the middle of Santa Clara Pueblo. She listens to the sounds of the morning as she greets the rising sun and asks for strength to be a good person. Gia Rose looks across the plaza and beyond the houses of the pueblo, or village, to the low brown hills and the dark blue mountains. She is happy to live in such a beautiful place.

*The adobe houses (above) of Santa Clara Pueblo are built around an open plaza paved with hard dirt (right).*

Gia Rose can tell that it is going to be a very hot day in the pueblo. There will be no breeze to cool off the barren packed ground of the plaza or the walls of the houses, made of adobe (sun-dried mud). "It will be a good day to go to the mountains for clay," she says to herself.

Before the sun is very high in the sky, Gia Rose and some members of her large family are ready to go. There is 8-month-old Benito, one of Gia Rose's 17 great-grand-children, and his parents, Athena and Bill. Athena is one of Gia Rose's 22 grand-children. There is 5-year-old Devonna, another great-grandchild. Also in the group are Eliza and Zachary, 11-year-old twins, and their mother, Nora, one of Gia Rose's 7 daughters. Everyone is excited to be together—and to be going to the mountains.

*Gia Rose with her daughter Nora* (back row), *grandchildren Eliza and Zachary* (middle row), *and great-grandchild Devonna* (front)

Piling into a car and a truck, the family drives out of Santa Clara Pueblo. *Pueblo* is the Spanish word for "village." When the Spanish came into the Southwest from Mexico in the 1500s, they called the Indian villages they saw pueblos. The word also came to be used for the people who lived in the villages. In Tewa, the language of the people of Santa Clara, the word for "village" is *owingeh*. The Tewa word for "people" is *towa*.

12

*Opposite: The family visits Puye, an ancient pueblo near Santa Clara. Below: Many pueblos are located near the Rio Grande, which flows through central New Mexico.*

After they leave the *owingeh*, Gia Rose and her family cross the *posongeh* (the big water), called the Rio Grande River by the Spanish. The *posongeh* is important because there is not much water in the southwestern United States. The Rio Grande is the largest river in New Mexico. It brings water to the fields of the *towa*, who grow corn, beans, and squash, just as their ancestors did thousands of years ago. Gia Rose tells Devonna, who is sitting next to her in the car, that they are lucky to live so close to the strong, flowing water.

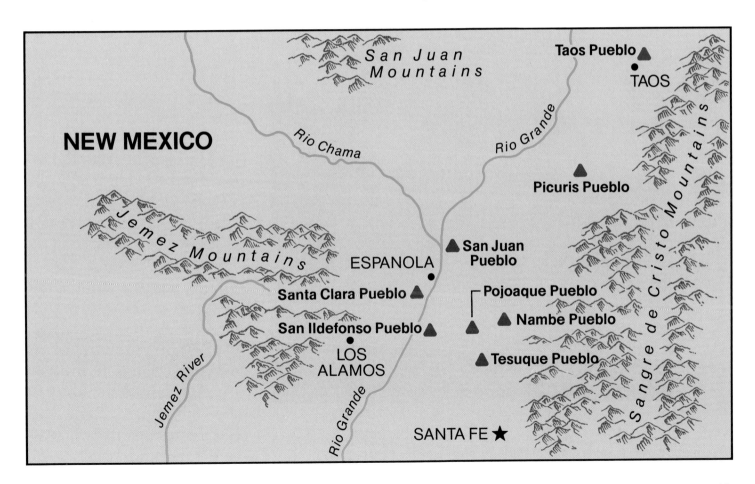

NEW MEXICO

San Juan Mountains

Rio Chama

Rio Grande

Taos Pueblo ▲
● TAOS

Picuris Pueblo ▲

Jemez Mountains

Sangre de Cristo Mountains

ESPANOLA ●

▲ San Juan Pueblo

Santa Clara Pueblo ▲

Pojoaque Pueblo ⌐

San Ildefonso Pueblo ▲

▲ ▲ Nambe Pueblo

LOS ALAMOS

Jemez River

▲ Tesuque Pueblo

Rio Grande

SANTA FE ★

*The ruins of San Geronimo Mission at Taos Pueblo. This mission church is one of many built at pueblos during the 1600s.*

A few miles along the road, they pass another *owingeh* called San Juan Pueblo. This is where the Spanish first lived when they came to the Southwest. They built a large Catholic church in San Juan, as they did in many other *owingehs*. They named the *owingehs* after Catholic saints like San Juan (Saint John). The Spanish wanted all the *towa* of the Southwest to think and be like them. But the *towa* had their own languages and ways of life. They did not want to be like the Spanish.

The people of San Juan speak Tewa, as do three other nearby *owingehs*. Gia Rose explains to Devonna that San Juan is just like Santa Clara because it also has a wide plaza from which you can see the hills and mountains and watch the clouds move across the sky. She talks about how the cloud spirits come from the mountains to bring rain to the *towa* and their crops.

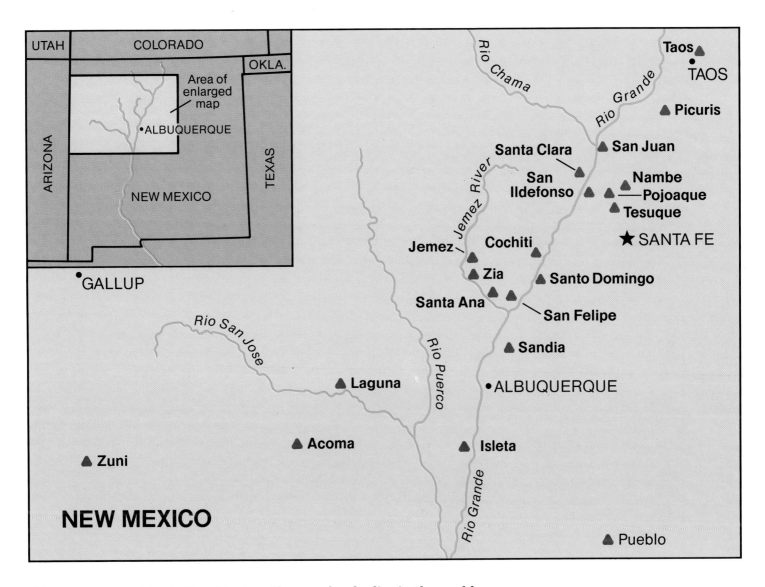

**NEW MEXICO**

*There are 19 pueblos in New Mexico. The people who live in the pueblos speak several different languages. In many of the villages along the Rio Grande, including Santa Clara and San Juan, the language is Tewa. The people of Taos speak a language called Tiwa. Keresan is spoken at Acoma and Laguna as well as at Santo Domingo and other pueblos near the Rio Grande. In western New Mexico, the people of Zuni have their own language.*

15

The mountains are far away from Santa Clara. It takes most of the morning to get to them. Gia Rose and her family leave the paved roads and ride along a narrow winding dirt road. When the car and truck stop, the children are ready to run and move their stiff legs. The grown-ups gather the shovels, picks, buckets, and tubs and begin walking to where they will dig clay. They call the children to follow. Eliza carries baby Benito in her arms as they walk around the low bushes and trees.

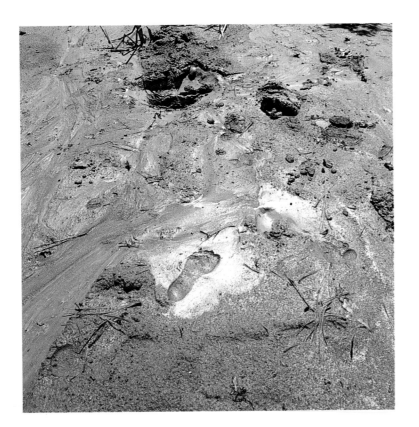

The clay pit is not far. Before they begin digging, Gia Rose stands quietly in front of the pit and talks to Clay-Old-Woman, who is the spirit of clay. Gia Rose tells Clay-Old-Woman that she has brought her family to get some clay. She says that they will work respectfully and carefully with the clay that they take. She thanks Clay-Old-Woman for being generous with herself.

After Gia Rose is finished, she nods her head, and Zachary, Eliza's twin brother, starts digging. Everyone helps to fill the buckets and tubs with clumps of sparkly brown-orange clay. Eliza helps by taking care of little Benito.

18

When the containers are filled, they are put in the truck. Then the children run to play in the cool stream. They splash and jump. What a good idea it was to come to the mountains! Afterwards, they eat their lunch in a shady place under a tree while Gia Rose tells them the story of Water-Jar-Boy.

*Devonna listens as Gia Rose tells the story of Water-Jar-Boy.*

19

W ater-Jar-Boy was born as a clay water jar. He grew up with all the other children of the pueblo and wanted to do whatever they did. One day his grandfather was going rabbit-hunting. Water-Jar-Boy begged to go with him. Grandfather said, "You have no arms or legs. You cannot walk or hunt." Water-Jar-Boy told his grandfather that he could roll even though he couldn't walk. So Grandfather agreed to take him.

When they came to a low hill, Grandfather placed Water-Jar-Boy on his side and gave him a gentle shove. Water-Jar-Boy rolled and rolled until he crashed into a

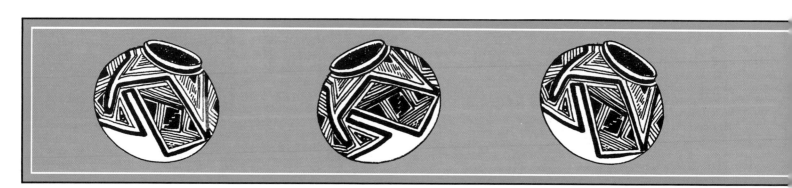

rock. He broke into many pieces, and in the midst of the pieces sat a young boy! The boy ran and hid behind a tree.

When Grandfather reached the bottom of the hill, he could not find his grandson. He was getting worried when he heard a voice calling "Grandfather, Grandfather, here I am." Grandfather was surprised when he saw a boy coming from behind a tree. The boy was smiling. When the boy explained who he was, Grandfather was very happy. Hand in hand, they hurried back to the pueblo so everybody could see that Water-Jar-Boy was a real boy with arms and legs.

*When they get back to the village, Eliza and her mother, Nora, pick out sticks and stones from the clay.*

After the story, the family is ready for the long drive back home. The children fall asleep in the car while the grown-ups talk about things going on in the *owingeh*. When they get back to Gia Rose's house, it is late afternoon and everyone is tired. But before they go to their own houses, they help to pick the large sticks and stones out of the clay. Then Zachary pours water into the buckets and tubs of clay. The clay will be set aside for a few days to slowly soak up the water.

Several days later, Gia Rose and two of her daughters, Judy and Tessie, do more work on the clay. They sit outside Gia Rose's house in the middle of the *owingeh* and push the wet clay through screens to take out small rocks and twigs. Devonna sits next to her great-grandfather, Michael, Gia Rose's husband. She watches and waits for someone to ask for water or another scraper, or to go answer the telephone.

Left: *Baby Benito plays by a bucket of clay.* Above: *After soaking in water, the hard, dry lumps of clay will be transformed into a soft, smooth material that can be molded and shaped.*

After the clay is cleaned, fine white sand must be mixed into it. This will keep the clay from cracking during the drying process. Mixing in the sand is a big job. Judy and Tessie take turns working the sand into the clay with their bare feet. Finally, the work is done, and the clay is wrapped in a cloth and set aside to rest for about a week.

When the clay is ready, some of the children and grown-ups of Gia Rose's family get together. They laugh and talk while they coil, pinch, press, and smooth the clay to make bowls and figures of animals and people.

Eliza rolls out slabs of clay with a rolling pin. She puts the slabs together to make a big creature with sticks coming out of its head. Devonna shapes lumps of clay to make a pair of hands ready to hold something. Micah, another cousin, rolls ropes of clay to make big and small snakes.

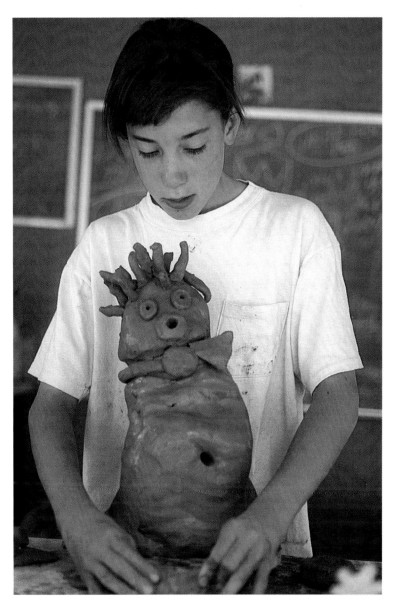

*Using slabs of clay, Eliza makes a big figure with sticks on its head.*

*Micah and his clay snakes*

Arin, Micah's sister, works carefully on a small bowl. She forms the sides of the bowl by coiling ropes of clay around and around. The adults also play with the clay. Gia Rose makes a frog, while Eliza and Zachary's mother, Nora, creates figures of a mother with her two naughty children. Rina, Devonna's grandmother, makes a small cup.

While they work, Gia Rose tells the children about Clay-Old-Woman. She says that Clay-Old-Woman lies within the earth and the clay. If people talk to her with respect, she will help them to create beautiful things. Gia Rose says that the pots and figures they make will be alive because Clay-Old-Woman will continue to live and breathe inside of them. In order to know that Clay-Old-Woman is breathing within their pieces, they must be quiet and listen. As they work, the children can feel Clay-Old-Woman in their hands.

*Aunt Tessie makes a coiled pot. She winds ropes of clay around and around on a base to form the sides of the pot. The coils are then pinched and scraped together to create a smooth surface.*

*After the clay pieces have dried, they must be made smooth by rubbing them with sandpaper.*

When they finish coiling and forming the clay, everyone carefully puts the pieces out of the way to dry. Big pieces like Nora's figures are wrapped in cloth so that they don't dry too fast and crack. The children know not to touch the clay pieces while they are drying because they are very fragile and will break easily.

A week later, it is time to smooth the pieces with sandpaper. Eliza is very careful as she helps to sand the hands that Devonna made. She sits working with her grandmother Rose, her aunt Rina, and her aunt Tessie, while the younger children play close by.

Sanding the pieces is hard work. Children quickly get tired of doing it, but 11-year-old Eliza works as hard as the adults. Old Great-grandfather Michael loves to sit and watch everyone at work. Ten years ago, before he had a stroke, he helped to sand the pots and put designs on them. He also helped to dig the clay, as Pueblo men usually do.

*Great-grandfather Michael watches as Aunt Rina, Gia Rose, and Eliza sand their pots and figures.*

When the pieces are as smooth as possible, Gia Rose takes out her special polishing stones. Some of the stones are special because her grandmother or aunts gave them to her. Others she found in special places. All the stones are special because they are hard and smooth, and when they are rubbed against the pots, they make the pots shiny.

Before the polishing begins, the pieces are coated with a thin, wet clay called slip. Then the children pick up the stones and begin to polish their figures and pots. Their hands move quickly before the wet slip dries. They work quietly because they have to pay close attention to what they are doing.

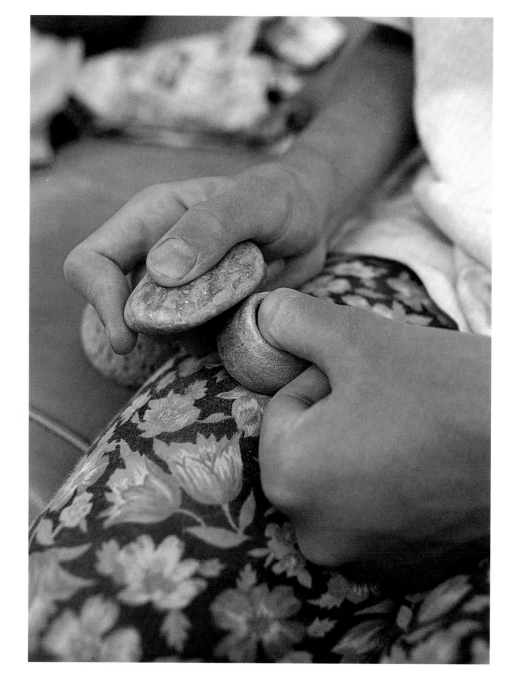

*Eliza uses a polishing stone to give a shiny finish to a small pot. The stone was given to Gia Rose by her grandmother.*

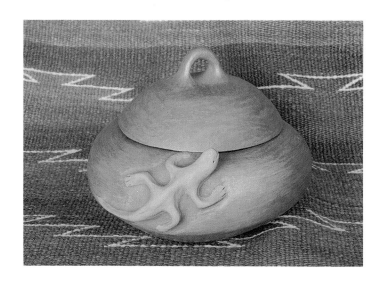

After each piece is finished, Gia Rose admires it. She talks about how pretty it is and about what design might be put on it. Gia Rose decides to put a lizard on one of her pieces. She will use wet slip to paint the lizard onto the polished surface with a brush. Sometimes she forms a lizard figure out of clay and attaches it to the piece before it is dried. Gia Rose knows many ways to design and decorate pottery.

Eliza decides not to put anything on her piece. Aunt Tessie likes the shiny polish on one of her pots and also decides not to put a design on it. Other pieces are painted with cloud, mountain, bear, lizard, and water-snake symbols. These designs have been used by the Santa Clara *towa* for hundreds of years.

The bear-paw design is used to help make the pot strong and remind people of the healing powers of the bear. The lizard is respected for the way it moves quickly over the ground. Both the clouds and the mountains are symbols of rain, for which the *towa* are always thankful. The water snake reminds people to be respectful of flowing water like the *posongeh*.

*Some traditional Santa Clara pottery designs include the lizard (top left), the water serpent (top right), and the bear paw (above).*

Another morning some weeks later, the family gathers again, this time to fire the pots and pieces. At each gathering, different members of the family are present. Pueblo people work in this way. They help each other make, sand, polish, and fire pots, but the same people seldom do all the work. The group changes, but the pottery-making process remains the same.

Firing makes the clay strong so that the pieces will not melt again or break easily. It can happen almost anywhere that a fire can be built. This time it is being done at the house of Devonna's grandmother Rina. Great-aunt Tessie is one of the oldest women present and is in charge of the firing. Devonna will help her.

The firing process is exciting because if it is not done right, many pieces may break. To get ready, Devonna and Great-aunt Tessie carefully set the pieces on a metal rack in the pit where the fire will be built. Great-aunt Tessie puts a metal cover over the pieces so that the fire will not burn directly on them. Devonna helps to stack wood slabs around the cover.

*Devonna places pottery on the rack in the firing pit.*

The fire is started. As the wood burns, everyone watches and listens for popping and cracking sounds. These sounds mean that something has cracked or exploded in the fire. They ask Clay-Old-Woman to help the pots live through the fire.

It seems like a long time before the fire burns out and the pieces can be seen. The grown-ups and children gather to find out what has broken. There are usually some broken pieces, but there are always some good pots and figures too. Devonna is excited about a tiny black water jar with two spouts. A large jar of this kind is used in wedding ceremonies. Members of one family drink water that has been blessed out of one spout, and members of the other family drink from the second spout. Afterwards, the water jar is shattered so that the bond between the bride and groom and their families will never be broken.

Many years ago, the *towa* of Santa Clara and the other *owingehs* made pottery only for their own use—for cooking, eating, or storage. These days the pottery of Santa Clara is highly valued, and many people want to buy it. Some of the pots and figures fired today will be given to friends or family members. Most of the pieces will be sold to visitors or traders who come to the *owingeh*. Others will be sold to art galleries and stores in places nearby or far away.

*The people of Santa Clara make figures of animals and people as well as clay jars and pots.*

35

The children of Santa Clara also sell their pots and figures. Devonna and her cousin Arin set up a table outside Gia Rose's house. They put up a sign that reads "Frogs for Sale" and wait for people to come and buy pots, frogs, and other small figures. There are always many tourists visiting Santa Clara Pueblo, so it is not too long before the children sell a frog.

Although many things are changing at Santa Clara Pueblo, pottery-making is still much the same as in the past. It still happens mostly outdoors and is done completely by hand. Making pottery helps children like Eliza, Zachary, Devonna, Arin, and Micah remember the place, the mountains, and the sky as they work and play in clay with their mothers, aunts, grandmothers, and great-grandmothers. It helps them to remember that they are all children of Clay-Old-Woman.

# Word List

**adobe** *(uh-DOH-bee)*—a building material made of mud or clay mixed with straw. Many Pueblo people construct their houses out of sun-dried adobe bricks.

**Clay-Old-Woman**—the spirit of clay, who lives within the earth. If potters treat the clay with respect, Clay-Old-Woman lives on in the pottery they make.

**coiling**—a method of making pottery by using long ropes of clay that are coiled around and around to create the sides of a pot

**firing**—putting clay pieces in a fire so that they will become hard

**Gia** *(GHEE-uh)*—the Tewa word for "mother"

**owingeh** *(oh-WIN-geh)*—the Tewa word for "village"

**plaza**—an open area in the center of a village

**polishing stones**—hard, smooth stones that are rubbed against a pot to make it shiny

**posongeh** *(poh-SON-geh)*—a Tewa word meaning "big water," used to refer to the Rio Grande River

**Pueblo** *(PWEH-bloh)*—Native American people who live in villages in the southwestern United States. Pueblo people speak several different languages but share many customs and ways of life.

**pueblo**—the Spanish word for "village," used for the Native American settlements of the Southwest and for the people who lived in them

**slip**—clay mixed with water to form a thin liquid. Slip is used to coat a piece of pottery before it is polished. Sometimes designs are also painted with slip.

**Tewa** *(TAY-wah)*—the language spoken by the people of Santa Clara Pueblo

**towa** *(TOE-wah)*—the Tewa word for "people"

# For Further Reading

Arnold, Caroline. *The Ancient Cliff Dwellers of Mesa Verde*. New York: Clarion Books, 1992.

D'Apice, Mary. *The Pueblo*. Vero Beach, Florida: Rourke Publications, 1990.

Hoyt-Goldsmith, Diane. *Pueblo Storyteller*. New York: Holiday House, 1991.

Keegan, Marcia. *Pueblo Boy: Growing Up in Two Worlds*. New York: Cobblehill Books/Dutton, 1991.

Liptak, Karen. *Indians of the Southwest*. New York: Facts on File, 1991.

Petersen, David. *The Anasazi*. Chicago: Childrens Press, 1991.

Trimble, Stephen. *The Village of Blue Stone*. New York: Macmillan Publishing Company, 1990.

Warren, Scott. *Cities in the Sand: The Ancient Civilizations of the Southwest*. San Francisco: Chronicle Books, 1992.

### We Are Still Here: Native Americans Today

*Children of Clay: A Family of Pueblo Potters*
*Clambake: A Wampanoag Tradition*
*Drumbeat...Heartbeat: A Celebration of the Powwow*
*Ininatig's Gift of Sugar: Traditional Native Sugarmaking*
*Kinaaldá: A Navajo Girl Grows Up*
*The Sacred Harvest: Ojibway Wild Rice Gathering*
*Shannon: An Ojibway Dancer*
*Songs from the Loom: A Navajo Girl Learns to Weave*

### About the Illustrations

The illustrations in this book are based on designs of Native American pottery from the Southwest. Traditional Pueblo designs include the water serpent (page 5), clouds (page 6), mountains (page 9), feathers (page 16), the bear paw (page 22), and the lizard (page 35). The figures on pages 20 and 21 are taken from ancient Southwestern pottery. The rabbit is adapted from designs on pots made by the Mimbres people, who lived in southwestern New Mexico about 1,000 years ago. The illustration of the water jar is based on a real water jar found in a ruined Anasazi village. The Anasazi, who built large pueblos in New Mexico and Arizona during the 1100s and 1200s, are the ancestors of the modern Pueblo Indians.

# About the Contributors

**Rina Swentzell** comes from a large family of potters at Santa Clara Pueblo in New Mexico. A potter herself, Rina is also a writer and educator specializing in the history and culture of Native Americans. She attended school in New Mexico, receiving an M.A. in Architecture and a Ph.D. in American Studies from the University of New Mexico. Rina Swentzell has held teaching positions at the University of New Mexico, the College of Santa Fe, and the Albuquerque Indian School and has been a guest lecturer at many institutions, including Syracuse University and the University of California. She has served as a consultant for the Smithsonian Institution's Museum of the American Indian and for public television's NOVA series. Her publications include numerous articles in southwestern journals on Pueblo culture and architecture. Rina lives in Santa Fe, New Mexico.

**Bill Steen** is a photographer and consultant whose work focuses on the culture and environment of the Southwest. For more than 20 years, he has served as a consultant in community development programs for both profit and nonprofit organizations. His recent projects have concentrated on ways of living in a dryland environment, including the creation of gardens and houses suited for the southwestern United States as well as Mexico. Bill's photographs of the Southwest have appeared in magazines and books. He lives in Canelo, Arizona, with his wife, Athena, who is from Santa Clara Pueblo.

Series Consultant **W. Roger Buffalohead**, Ponca, has been involved in Indian Education for more than 20 years, serving as a national consultant on issues of Indian curricula and tribal development. He has a B.A. in American History from Oklahoma State University and an M.A. from the University of Wisconsin, Madison. Buffalohead has taught at the University of Cincinnati, the University of California, Los Angeles, and the University of Minnesota, where he was director of the American Indian Learning and Resources Center from 1986 to 1991. Currently he teaches at the American Indian Arts Institute in Santa Fe, New Mexico. Among his many activities, Buffalohead is a founding board member of the National Indian Education Association and a member of the Cultural Concerns Committee of the National Conference of American Indians. He lives in Santa Fe.

Series Consultant **Juanita G. Corbine Espinosa**, Dakota/Ojibway, serves as director of Native Arts Circle, Minnesota's first statewide Native American arts agency. She is first and foremost a community organizer, active in a broad range of issues, many of which are related to the importance of art in community life. In addition, she is a board member of the Minneapolis American Indian Center and an advisory member of the Minnesota State Arts Board's Cultural Pluralism Task Force. She was one of the first people to receive the state's McKnight Human Service Award. She lives in Minneapolis.